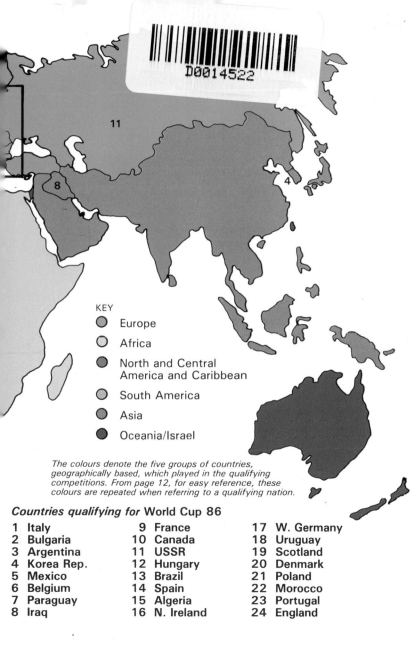

D0014522

KEY

- ⬤ Europe
- ◯ Africa
- ⬤ North and Central America and Caribbean
- ◯ South America
- ⬤ Asia
- ⬤ Oceania/Israel

The colours denote the five groups of countries, geographically based, which played in the qualifying competitions. From page 12, for easy reference, these colours are repeated when referring to a qualifying nation.

Countries qualifying for World Cup 86

1 Italy	9 France	17 W. Germany
2 Bulgaria	10 Canada	18 Uruguay
3 Argentina	11 USSR	19 Scotland
4 Korea Rep.	12 Hungary	20 Denmark
5 Mexico	13 Brazil	21 Poland
6 Belgium	14 Spain	22 Morocco
7 Paraguay	15 Algeria	23 Portugal
8 Iraq	16 N. Ireland	24 England

Keep your own record of the World Cup '86 competition, as each round is played.

Contents

Acknowledgments:
Photographs of World Cup trophy on front and back cover ©FIFA 1974.
Photograph on page 10 ©GAMMA supplied by Frank Spooner Pictures.

Details contained in this book were correct at the time of going to press.

British Library Cataloguing in Publication Data
Baker, John P. (John Peter)
  World Cup '86.
  1. World Cup. *(Football championship : 1986 : Mexico)*
  —Juvenile literature
  I. Title
  796.334'66   GV943.5 1986
  ISBN 0-7214-0944-X

First edition

Published by Ladybird Books Ltd Loughborough Leicestershire UK
Ladybird Books Inc Lewiston Maine 04240 USA

WORLD CUP 86

written by JOHN P. BAKER
designed by CHRIS REED
photographs by GEORGE HERRINGSHAW

Ladybird Books

History

The Olympic Games provided world competition for amateur footballers but as the professional game grew throughout the world, FIFA, the organisation concerned with the administration of international football, wanted an equivalent competition for professional footballers.

After ten years of discussion and planning, Jules Rimet, the president of the French Football Association and of FIFA, saw his dreams become reality with the staging of the 1930 World Cup finals in Uruguay.

Thirteen teams travelled from different parts of the world for the first World Cup competition. No British teams took part because they were not members of FIFA at the time.

Out of respect for all the work Jules Rimet had done to launch the competition, FIFA decided to name the trophy the *Jules Rimet Cup*. It was solid gold, 30 cm high and it weighed just over 4 kilograms.

World travel is very quick and easy nowadays but it has not always been so. It could take two months for a team to travel to the host country, play in the competition and then travel back.

In 1934 and 1938 the whole competition was run on a knock-out basis and in 1934 the USA, Argentina and Brazil travelled all the way to Italy for just one match. Since 1950, when the World Cup finals were held again after a break of twelve years, different ways have been tried to give each team more games.

The 1982 finals involved twenty-four teams for the first time ever. Again in 1986 twenty-four teams are involved but the arrangement for the later stages has been amended to include a quarter final competition.

The *Jules Rimet Cup* was played for until 1970 when Brazil, having won it three times, was allowed to keep it forever. The new FIFA trophy is solid gold, 36 cm high and is simply called the *World Cup*. It was designed by an Italian and was selected from fifty-three entries. The *World Cup* was used for the first time in 1974.

Pele (Brazil) holding the Jules Rimet Cup *with Seeler (W. Germany) holding the* World Cup

Previous World Cup competitions

Country	*F	Won	R/up	3rd	4th
Brazil	12	1958 1962 1970	1950	1938 1978	1974
Italy	10	1934 1938 1982	1970		1978
West Germany (° as Germany)	10	1954 1974	1966 1982	1934° 1970	1958
Mexico	8				
Argentina	8	1978	1930		
Hungary	8		1938 1954		
France	8			1958	1982
Uruguay	7	1930 1950			1954 1970
England	7	1966			
Sweden	7		1958	1950	1938
Czechoslovakia	7		1934 1962		
Yugoslavia	7			1930§	1962
Spain	6				1950
Switzerland	6				
Belgium	6				
Chile	6			1962	
USSR	5				1966
Scotland	5				
Austria	5			1954	1934
Holland	4		1974 1978		
Poland	4			1974 1982	
Bulgaria	4				
Rumania	4				
Peru	4				

* = *Finals* § 1930 Yugoslavia and USA shared 3rd place

51 different countries have participated in the 12 World Cup final competitions held so far.

Countries qualifying three times
USA (joint 3rd place 1930), Paraguay

Countries qualifying twice
Northern Ireland, El Salvador

Countries qualifying once
Egypt, Cuba, Norway, Dutch East Indies, Turkey, Korea, Colombia, Wales, Portugal (3rd place 1966), Israel, Morocco, Haiti, Iran, Zaïre, East Germany, Tunisia, North Korea, Australia, Cameroon, Algeria, Kuwait, Honduras, New Zealand

Finals since 1930

Venue	Finalists			Venue	Finalists		
1930 Uruguay	Uruguay 4	v :	Argentina 2	1962 Chile	Brazil 3	v :	Czecho'vakia 1
1934 Italy	Italy 2 (1 – 1) before	v : extra time	Czecho'vakia 1	1966 England	England 4 (2 – 2) before	v : extra time	W. Germany 2
1938 France	Italy 4	v :	Hungary 2	1970 Mexico	Brazil 4	v :	Italy 1
No Competition during the War years				1974 W. Germany	W. Germany 2	v :	Holland 1
1950 Brazil	Final Pool Uruguay 5 points	v :	Brazil 4 points	1978 Argentina	Argentina 3	v :	Holland 1
1954 Switzerland	W. Germany 3	v :	Hungary 2	1982 Spain	Italy 3	v :	W. Germany 1
1958 Sweden	Brazil 5	v :	Sweden 2				

Rossi of Italy scores in the 1982 World Cup final against W. Germany

The host nation 1986 – Mexico

A piece of World Cup history will be made as the final competition returns to a previous host country. Mexico staged the 1970 World Cup finals when Brazil beat Italy to win the *Jules Rimet Cup* outright, having won it three times. The opportunity to stage the finals again this year arose because Colombia withdrew.

The qualifying competition kicked off in Nicosia on 2nd May 1984 when Cyprus were beaten 2 – 1 by Austria. Nineteen months later on 4th December 1985 the final place was decided in Australia.

A poster commemorating the 1930 World Cup in Uruguay

Uruguay's win over Chile gave them their first chance since 1974 to repeat their earlier World Championships of 1930 and 1950.

The final competition in Mexico will be staged in nine cities using 12 stadiums. The opening match will be in the Azteca Stadium in Mexico City on 31st May. The final match in the same stadium, four weeks later, will decide the World Champions 1986. Will the host country once more provide the winner? Out of the 12 competitions staged to date, the host nation has taken the trophy five times (Uruguay, Italy, England, West Germany and Argentina).

The stadiums for World Cup final competitions seem to get bigger and better as host countries develop venues which will continue to provide facilities long after the

Souvenir stalls outside the Azteca Stadium, Mexico City

competition has moved away. The Querétaro Stadium, inaugurated on 5th February 1985 with a match between Mexico and Poland, is really quite magnificent. The Cuahtémoc Stadium in Puebla is also interesting in that it has a ground drainage system which stores up to 7000 cubic metres of water in a subterranean basin to be purified and recycled for use within the stadium's showers and toilets, etc.

The final match of the 1982 competition was watched by one billion viewers all over the world. A special centre has been built in Mexico City to house the world's press and television. It has eight floors, four below ground and four above. The 52 matches over the 30-day programme will receive plenty of coverage.

A further historic but tragic event occurred on 19th September 1985. Mexico suffered its worst-ever earthquake. Although the tremors were felt over a 310,000 mile area, it was the capital which suffered the most damage. It will be well into 1986 before the city begins to return to normal but since most of the stadiums are outside this area both FIFA and the Mexican authorities agreed that the World Cup competition could go ahead.

Part of the damage caused by the earthquake

Qualifying competitions

FIFA has 150 Associations affiliated and of these 123 countries have taken part in the present competition. To decide which 22 countries were to contest the 1986 finals, plus World Champions Italy and host country Mexico, public draws were made for the preliminary rounds in the six continents.

South America provided ten entries. They were arranged in three leagues with the champions of each qualifying for Mexico and runners-up playing a cup competition to provide the fourth qualifier.

The seventeen North/Central America and Caribbean (Concacaf) countries were arranged into three groups for a home and away cup competition, producing nine teams for a league in three groups. The third round between these league champions was also played on a league basis with the winner qualifying to join Mexico in the finals.

Europe had thirty-two entries in seven groups of four or five countries, playing in leagues. The five-team leagues had winners and runners-up qualifying for Mexico. The four-team leagues only guaranteed a place for the winner. The runner-up had to win in a two-leg play-off to qualify. Italy automatically qualified as World Champions.

There were twenty-seven entries from the Asian group. Four groups, with two sub groups in each, provided eight teams. There were two knock-out rounds and finally the third round winners both qualified for Mexico.

Twenty-nine African countries entered their qualifying competition. Four rounds of cup competitions on a home and away basis eventually produced the two representatives of the group in the final competition.

Oceania and Israel had four entries in the competition. The four countries played in a league with the champions playing the runner-up of the European group 7 on a home and away basis. On 4th December 1985 the final match made Scotland the 24th qualifier and left the Oceania/Israel group without a representative in the final competition.

Italy raise the World Cup *as Champions in 1982*

South America

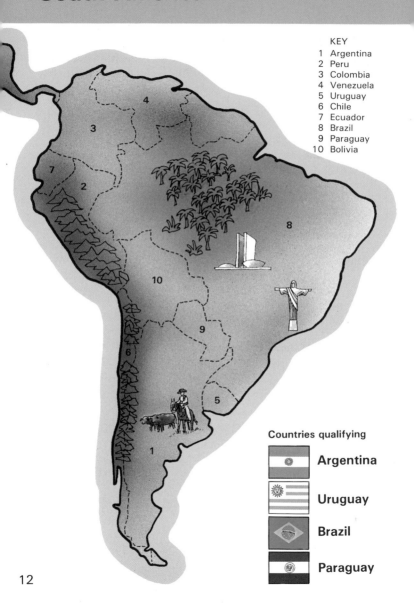

KEY
1 Argentina
2 Peru
3 Colombia
4 Venezuela
5 Uruguay
6 Chile
7 Ecuador
8 Brazil
9 Paraguay
10 Bolivia

Countries qualifying

Argentina

Uruguay

Brazil

Paraguay

1st Round
League competition played on a home and away basis.
Champions of each group qualify for Mexico.
Teams in bold type qualify for next round.

GROUP 1	P	W	D	L	F:A	Pts
Argentina	6	4	1	1	12:6	9
Peru	6	3	2	1	8:4	8
Colombia	6	2	2	2	6:6	6
Venezuela	6	0	1	5	5:15	1

GROUP 2	P	W	D	L	F:A	Pts
Uruguay	4	3	0	1	6:4	6
Chile	4	2	1	1	10:5	5
Ecuador	4	0	1	3	4:11	1

GROUP 3	P	W	D	L	F:A	Pts
Brazil	4	2	2	0	6:2	6
Paraguay	4	1	2	1	5:4	4
Bolivia	4	0	2	2	2:7	2

2nd Round
Cup competition played on a home and away basis.
Winning team qualifies for Mexico.

Paraguay	v	Colombia
3	:	0
1	:	2

Chile	v	Peru
4	:	2
1	:	0

Paraguay	v	Chile
3	:	0
2	:	2

'Pique' – the official mascot of the FIFA World Cup 1986
© Sport-Billy Productions 1984

13

North/Central America and Caribbean (Concacaf)

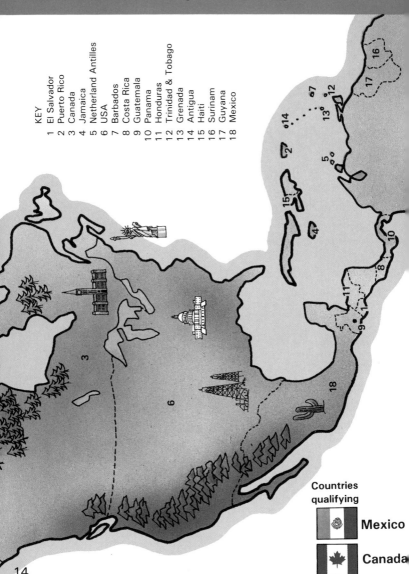

KEY
1 El Salvador
2 Puerto Rico
3 Canada
4 Jamaica
5 Netherland Antilles
6 USA
7 Barbados
8 Costa Rica
9 Guatemala
10 Panama
11 Honduras
12 Trinidad & Tobago
13 Grenada
14 Antigua
15 Haiti
16 Surinam
17 Guyana
18 Mexico

Countries qualifying

Mexico

Canada

1st Round
Cup competition played on a home and away basis.
Teams in bold type qualify for next round.

GROUP 1

El Salvador	v	Puerto Rico
5	:	0
3	:	0

Canada	v	Jamaica (expelled)

Netherland Antilles	v	**USA**
0	:	0
0	:	4

GROUP 2

Barbados (withdrew)	v	**Costa Rica**

Guatemala – walkover

Panama	v	**Honduras**
0	:	3
0	:	1

GROUP 3

Trinidad & Tobago	v	Grenada (withdrew)

Antigua	v	**Haiti**
0	:	4
2	:	1

Surinam	v	Guyana
1	:	0
1	:	1

2nd Round
Rounds 2 and 3 are league competitions played on a home and away basis.
Teams in bold type qualify for next round.

GROUP 1	P	W	D	L	F:A	Pts
Honduras	4	2	2	0	5:3	6
El Salvador	4	2	1	1	7:2	5
Surinam	4	0	1	3	2:9	1

GROUP 2	P	W	D	L	F:A	Pts
Canada	4	3	1	0	7:2	7
Guatemala	4	2	1	1	7:3	5
Haiti	4	0	0	4	0:9	0

GROUP 3	P	W	D	L	F:A	Pts
Costa Rica	4	2	2	0	6:2	6
USA	4	2	1	1	4:3	5
Trinidad & Tobago	4	0	1	3	2:7	1

3rd Round
Team in bold type qualifies for the finals.

	P	W	D	L	F:A	Pts
Canada	4	2	2	0	4:2	6
Honduras	4	1	1	2	6:6	3
Costa Rica	4	0	3	1	4:6	3

Mexico qualify for finals as host country

Europe

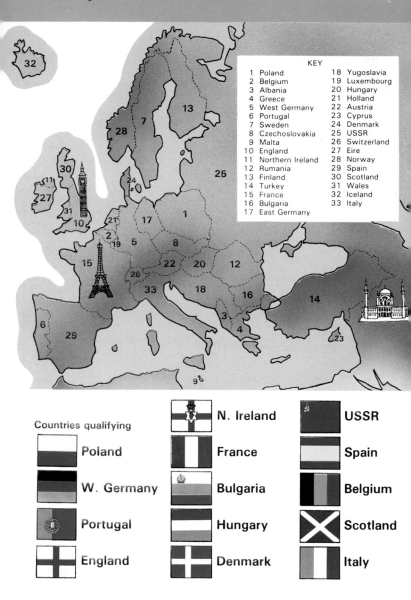

KEY

1	Poland	18	Yugoslavia
2	Belgium	19	Luxembourg
3	Albania	20	Hungary
4	Greece	21	Holland
5	West Germany	22	Austria
6	Portugal	23	Cyprus
7	Sweden	24	Denmark
8	Czechoslovakia	25	USSR
9	Malta	26	Switzerland
10	England	27	Eire
11	Northern Ireland	28	Norway
12	Rumania	29	Spain
13	Finland	30	Scotland
14	Turkey	31	Wales
15	France	32	Iceland
16	Bulgaria	33	Italy
17	East Germany		

Countries qualifying

Poland

W. Germany

Portugal

England

N. Ireland

France

Bulgaria

Hungary

Denmark

USSR

Spain

Belgium

Scotland

Italy

Qualifying Competitions

League competition played on a home and away basis.

Champions of each group qualify for Mexico.
Runners-up in the larger groups 2, 3, 4 and 6 also qualify for Mexico.
Teams in bold type qualify for play-offs on a home and away basis.

GROUP 1	P	W	D	L	F:A	Pts
Poland	6	3	2	1	10:6	8
Belgium	6	3	2	1	7:3	8
Albania	6	1	2	3	6:9	4
Greece	6	1	2	3	5:10	4

GROUP 5	P	W	D	L	F:A	Pts
Hungary	6	5	0	1	12:4	10
Holland	6	3	1	2	11:5	7
Austria	6	3	1	2	9:8	7
Cyprus	6	0	0	6	3:18	0

GROUP 2	P	W	D	L	F:A	Pts
W. Germany	8	5	2	1	22:9	12
Portugal	8	5	0	3	12:10	10
Sweden	8	4	1	3	14:9	9
Czecho'vakia	8	3	2	3	11:12	8
Malta	8	0	1	7	6:25	1

GROUP 6	P	W	D	L	F:A	Pts
Denmark	8	5	1	2	17:6	11
USSR	8	4	2	2	13:8	10
Switzerland	8	2	4	2	5:10	8
Eire	8	2	2	4	5:10	6
Norway	8	1	3	4	4:10	5

GROUP 3	P	W	D	L	F:A	Pts
England	8	4	4	0	21:2	12
N. Ireland	8	4	2	2	8:5	10
Rumania	8	3	3	2	12:7	9
Finland	8	3	2	3	7:12	8
Turkey	8	0	1	7	2:24	1

GROUP 7	P	W	D	L	F:A	Pts
Spain	6	4	0	2	9:8	8
Scotland	6	3	1	2	8:4	7
Wales	6	3	1	2	7:6	7
Iceland	6	1	0	5	4:10	2

GROUP 4	P	W	D	L	F:A	Pts
France	8	5	1	2	15:4	11
Bulgaria	8	5	1	2	13:5	11
E. Germany	8	5	0	3	16:9	10
Yugoslavia	8	3	2	3	7:8	8
Luxembourg	8	0	0	8	2:27	0

PLAY-OFFS (for place in the final)

Belgium	v	Holland
1	:	0
1	:	2

Belgium qualify on away goal rule

Scotland	v	Australia (winners of Oceania group)
2	:	0
0	:	0

Italy qualify as 1982 World Champions

Asia

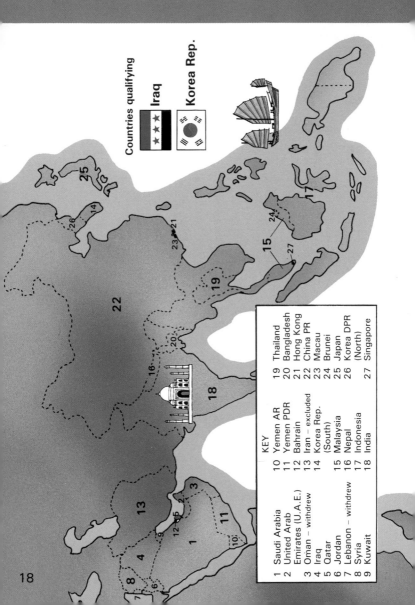

Countries qualifying

Iraq

Korea Rep.

KEY

1 Saudi Arabia
2 United Arab
   Emirates (U.A.E.)
3 Oman – withdrew
4 Iraq
5 Qatar
6 Jordan
7 Lebanon – withdrew
8 Syria
9 Kuwait
10 Yemen AR
11 Yemen PDR
12 Bahrain
13 Iran – excluded
14 Korea Rep.
   (South)
15 Malaysia
16 Nepal
17 Indonesia
18 India
19 Thailand
20 Bangladesh
21 Hong Kong
22 China PR
23 Macau
24 Brunei
25 Japan
26 Korea DPR
   (North)
27 Singapore

Qualifying Competitions

1st Round
League competition played on a home and away basis.
Teams in bold type qualify for next round.

GROUP 1

Sub Grp. 1A	P	W	D	L	F:A	Pts
U.A.E.	2	1	1	0	1:0	3
Saudi Arabia	2	0	1	1	0:1	1
Oman withdrew						

Sub Grp. 1B	P	W	D	L	F:A	Pts
Iraq	4	3	0	1	7:6	6
Qatar	4	2	0	2	6:3	4
Jordan	4	1	0	3	3:7	2
Lebanon withdrew						

GROUP 2

Sub Grp. 2A	P	W	D	L	F:A	Pts
Syria	4	3	1	0	5:0	7
Kuwait	4	2	1	1	8:2	5
Yemen AR	4	0	0	4	1:12	0

Sub Grp. 2B	P	W	D	L	F:A	Pts
Bahrain	2	1	1	0	7:4	3
Yemen PDR	2	0	1	1	4:7	1
Iran excluded						

GROUP 3

Sub Grp. 3A	P	W	D	L	F:A	Pts
Korea Rep.	4	3	0	1	8:1	6
Malaysia	4	2	1	1	6:2	5
Nepal	4	0	1	3	0:11	1

Sub Grp. 3B	P	W	D	L	F:A	Pts
Indonesia	6	4	1	1	8:4	9
India	6	2	3	1	7:6	7
Thailand	6	1	2	3	4:4	4
Bangladesh	6	2	0	4	5:10	4

GROUP 4

Sub Grp. 4A	P	W	D	L	F:A	Pts
Hong Kong	6	5	1	0	19:2	11
China PR	6	4	1	1	23:2	9
Macau	6	2	0	4	4:15	4
Brunei	6	0	0	6	2:29	0

Sub Grp. 4B	P	W	D	L	F:A	Pts
Japan	4	3	1	0	9:1	7
Korea DPR	4	1	2	1	3:2	4
Singapore	4	0	1	3	2:11	1

Rounds 2 and 3 are cup competitions played on a home and away basis.
Teams in bold type qualify for next round.

2nd Round

U.A.E.	v	**Iraq**
2	:	3
2	:	1

Iraq qualify on away goal rule

Bahrain	v	**Syria**
1	:	1
0	:	1

Korea Rep.	v	Indonesia
2	:	0
4	:	1

Japan	v	Hong Kong
3	:	0
2	:	1

3rd Round
Winners qualify for Mexico.

Syria	v	**Iraq**
0	:	0
1	:	3

Japan	v	**Korea Rep.**
1	:	2
0	:	1

19

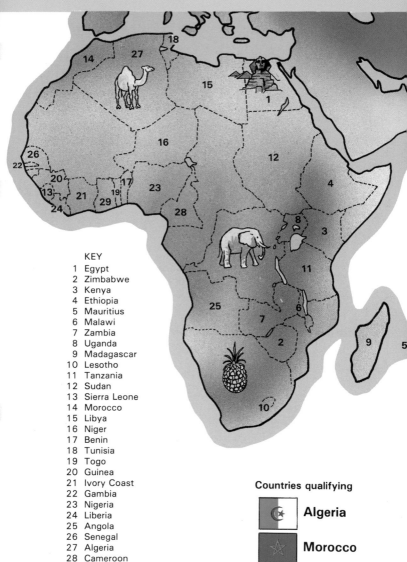

KEY
1. Egypt
2. Zimbabwe
3. Kenya
4. Ethiopia
5. Mauritius
6. Malawi
7. Zambia
8. Uganda
9. Madagascar
10. Lesotho
11. Tanzania
12. Sudan
13. Sierra Leone
14. Morocco
15. Libya
16. Niger
17. Benin
18. Tunisia
19. Togo
20. Guinea
21. Ivory Coast
22. Gambia
23. Nigeria
24. Liberia
25. Angola
26. Senegal
27. Algeria
28. Cameroon
29. Ghana

Countries qualifying

Algeria

Morocco

Qualifying Competitions

Each round is a cup competition played on a home and away basis.
Teams in bold type qualify for next round.

1st Round

Egypt	v	Zimbabwe
1	:	0
1	:	1

Kenya	v	Ethiopia
2	:	1
3	:	3

Mauritius	v	**Malawi**
0	:	1
0	:	4

Zambia	v	Uganda
3	:	0
0	:	1

Madagascar	v	Lesotho (excluded)

Tanzania	v	**Sudan**
1	:	1
0	:	0

Sudan qualify on away goals rule

Sierra Leone	v	**Morocco**
0	:	1
0	:	4

Libya	v	Niger (withdrew)

Benin	v	**Tunisia**
0	:	2
0	:	4

Togo (withdrew)	v	**Guinea**

Ivory Coast	v	Gambia
4	:	0
2	:	3

1st Round cont.

Nigeria	v	Liberia
3	:	0
1	:	0

Angola	v	Senegal
1	:	0
0	:	1

Angola qualify on penalty kicks

Walkovers
Algeria
Cameroon
Ghana

2nd Round

Zambia	v	Cameroon
4	:	1
1	:	1

Morocco	v	Malawi
2	:	0
0	:	0

Angola	v	**Algeria**
0	:	0
2	:	3

Kenya	v	**Nigeria**
0	:	3
1	:	3

Egypt	v	Madagascar
1	:	0
0	:	1

Egypt qualify on penalty kicks

Guinea	v	**Tunisia**
1	:	0
0	:	2

2nd Round cont.

Sudan	v	**Libya**
0	:	0
0	:	4

Ivory Coast	v	**Ghana**
0	:	0
0	:	2

3rd Round

Algeria	v	Zambia
2	:	0
1	:	0

Ghana	v	**Libya**
0	:	0
0	:	2

Nigeria	v	**Tunisia**
1	:	0
0	:	2

Egypt	v	**Morocco**
0	:	0
0	:	2

4th Round

Winning teams in bold type qualify for Mexico.

Tunisia	v	**Algeria**
1	:	4
0	:	3

Morocco	v	Libya
3	:	0
0	:	1

Oceania/Israel

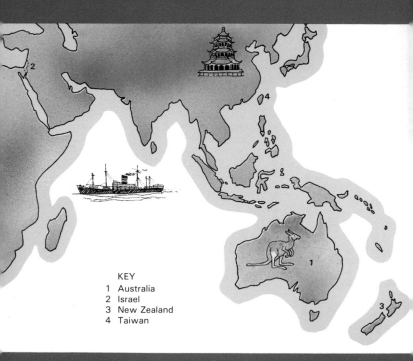

KEY
1 Australia
2 Israel
3 New Zealand
4 Taiwan

Qualifying Competitions

League competition played on a home and away basis.

	P	W	D	L	F:A	Pts
Australia	6	4	2	0	20:2	10
Israel	6	3	1	2	17:6	7
N. Zealand	6	3	1	2	13:4	7
Taiwan	6	0	0	6	1:36	0

Australia *to play runner-up of European group 7 on a home and away basis for a place in the finals. See page 17.*

Brazil

Country
Fifth biggest country in the world
Population 119 million
Capital Brasilia — built specially to be Brazil's new capital and is only about 30 years old.
Currency 100 centavos = 1 Cruzeiro

Team
Manager To be decided

Players to watch
Zico, Giovani, Falcao, Socrates, Casagrande

How they qualified
By leading Group 3 in the South American qualifying competition.

Team colours
Yellow, blue and white

Socrates

Previous appearances in finals
World Champions in 1958, 1962, 1970. Runners-up in 1950. Third place in 1938, 1978. Fourth place in 1974. By qualifying for these finals Brazil maintains its record of being the only country to appear in all World Cup finals.

Zico

23

Argentina

Diego Maradona

Country
Eighth biggest country in the world
Population 28 million
Capital Buenos Aires – sixth biggest city
in the world
Currency 100 centavos = 1 Austral

Team
Manager Carlos Bilardo

Players to watch
Passerella, Maradona

Team colours
Pale blue/white and black

Previous appearances in finals
Played in eight World Cup finals, winning as
host nation in 1978 and being beaten
finalists in the first-ever World Cup in 1930.

Uruguay

Country
Population 3 million
Capital Montevideo
Currency 100 centésimos = 1 New Uruguayan Peso

Team
Manager Omar Borras   *Player to watch* Francescoli

How they qualified
First nation to qualify for Mexico by winning Group 2 of the South
American competition. Winning all games except the away game
with Chile they scored 6 goals to 4 against them.

Team colours Pale blue and black

Previous appearances in finals
Hosted the first World Cup finals in 1930 and won. Also World
Champions in 1950 in Brazil. Fourth place in 1954 and 1970. This
is Uruguay's eighth World Cup final competition.

Paraguay

Country
Population 3 million
Capital Asunción
Currency 100 céntimos = 1 Guarani

Team
Manager Cayetano Re

Players to watch
Rogelio, Delgado, Cañete

How they qualified
Runners-up to Brazil in Group 3 of the South American qualifying competition. Won the cup system beating Chile 5 − 2 on aggregate in the final.

Team colours
Red/white and blue

Previous appearances in finals
Appeared in three World Cup final competitions but haven't yet got as far as the last four.

Mexico

Country
Population 67 million
Capital Mexico City − largest city in the world.
Currency 100 centavos = 1 Peso
Time in Mexico is six hours behind G.M.T

Team
Manager Bora Milutinovic

Players to watch
Amador, Flores, Boy, Sanchez

Team colours
Green, white and red

Thomas Boy

Canada

Country
Second largest country, covering
10 million square kilometres
Population 25 million
Capital Ottawa
Currency 100 cents = 1 Canadian
Dollar

Team
Manager Tony Waiters (former
England goalkeeper)

Players to watch
Ragan, Wilson, Valentine

Team colours
All red

*Carl Valentine – formerly of
West Bromwich Albion*

Belgium

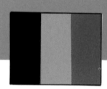

Country
Population 10 million
Capital Brussels
Currency 100 centimes = 1 Belgian franc

Team
Manager Guy Thys

Player to watch
Ceulemans, Scifo

How they qualified
Runners-up to Poland in European Group 1. Qualified for play-off
with Holland over two legs. This play-off was decided in Belgium's
favour on the away goal rule after a 2 – 2 aggregate score.

Team colours
All red

England

Country
Population 46 million
Capital London – ninth largest city in the world
Currency 100 pence = 1 pound Sterling

Team
Manager Bobby Robson

Bryan Robson

Players to watch
Wilkins, Shilton, Robson, Lineker

How they qualified
Unbeaten Champions of Group 3 in the European qualifying competition. They won four games and drew four, scoring 21 goals to 2 against.

Peter Shilton

Team colours
White and navy blue

Previous appearances in finals
Played in seven World Championships, winning once as host nation in 1966. That was the only occasion on which they got into the last four.

Northern Ireland

Country
Population 1.5 million
Capital Belfast
Currency 100 pence = 1 pound Sterling

Norman Whiteside

Team
Manager Billy Bingham – one of the four managers still in charge of a team since the last World Cup competition.

Players to watch
Jennings, Armstrong, McIlroy, Whiteside

Gerry Armstrong

How they qualified
Runners-up to England in European Group 3. They won four of their eight games and drew two, scoring 8 goals to 5 against them.

Team colours
Green and white

Scotland

Country
Population 5 million
Capital Edinburgh
Currency 100 pence = 1 pound Sterling

Team
Manager Alex Ferguson
Previous manager, Jock
Stein, died tragically at the
last of Scotland's group
matches.

Players to watch
Strachan, Souness,
McAvennie, Cooper

Gordon Strachan

Frank McAvennie

Team colours
Navy blue, white and red

Previous appearances in finals
Five previous World Cup
finals but no last four place to
show for it yet.

France

Country
Population 55 million
Capital Paris
Currency 100 centimes = 1 French franc

Team
Manager Henri Michel

Players to watch
Platini, Giresse

Team colours
Blue, white and red

Previous appearances in finals
Eight previous finals with third place in 1958 and fourth place in the last finals in 1982.

Italy

Country
Population 57 million
Capital Rome
Currency Lira

Team
Manager Enzo Bearzot, naturally still in the job after 1982's success in the competition.

Players to watch
Massaro, Cabrini

Team colours
Blue and white

Previous appearances in finals
Italy has the second best record in World Cup finals. Appearing in ten, winning in 1934 (hosts), 1938 and 1982. Runners-up in 1970 and fourth place in 1978.

Spain

Country
Population 38 million
Capital Madrid
Currency 100 céntimos = 1 Peseta

Team
Manager Miguel Muñoz

Player to watch
Butragueno

How they qualified
Champions of European Group 7. Winning four of their six matches and scoring 9 goals to 8 against.

Team colours
Red, blue and black

Previous appearances in finals
Appeared in six previous finals with a fourth place in 1950. They hosted the 1982 competition.

W.Germany

Country
Population 61 million
Capital Bonn
Currency 100 pfennig =
1 Deutsche Mark

Team
Manager Franz Beckenbauer

Players to watch Völler, Rummenigge

Team colours White and black

Previous appearances in finals
Of their ten previous appearances in the finals, they have been in the first four places seven times.

Karl-Heinz Rummenigge

Denmark

Country
Population 5 million
Capital Copenhagen
Currency 100 øre = 1 Danish Krone

Team
Manager Sepp Piontek

Players to watch
Olsen, Laudrup, Molby, Lerby

How they qualified
Champions of European Group 6.
Winning five of their eight games
and drawing one, scoring 17 goals
to 6 against them.

Team colours
Red and white

Sören Lerby

Poland

Country
Population 36 million
Capital Warsaw
Currency 100 Groszy = 1 Zloty

Team
Manager Antoni Piechniczek

Players to watch
Boniek, Zmuda

How they qualified
Champions of Group 1 in the European competition winning three
of their six games and drawing two. They scored 10 goals to 6
against.

Team colours
White and red

Hungary

Country
Population 11 million
Capital Budapest
Currency 100 Filler = 1 Florint

Team
Manager Gyorgy Mezey

Players to watch
Detari, Nyilasi

How they qualified
Champions of Group 5 in the European competition. Winning five of their six matches and losing only to Holland. They scored 12 goals to 4 against.

Team colours
Red, white and green

Previous appearances in finals
Hungary have qualified for eight previous finals and have been runners-up twice, in 1938 and 1954.

USSR

Rinat Dassayev

Country
Biggest country in the world, covering 22½ million square kilometres
Population 274 million – the third largest in the world behind China and India.
Capital Moscow – world's tenth largest city.
Currency 100 Kopeks = 1 Rouble

Team
Manager Eduard Malofeyev

Players to watch
Dassayev, Blokhin, Shengelia

Team colours
Red and white

Portugal

Country
Population 10 million
Capital Lisbon
Currency 100 centavos = 1 Portuguese Escudo

Team
Manager Jose Torres   *Players to watch* Gomes, Bento

Team colours Red and green

Previous appearances in finals
Qualified once before in 1966 when they took third place in England.

Bulgaria

Country
Population 9 million
Capital Sofia
Currency 100 Stotinki = 1 Lev

Team
Manager Voutsov   *Players to watch* Dimitrov, Guetov

Team colours White and green

Previous appearances in finals
Four previous appearances but yet to qualify for the four top positions.

Iraq

Country
Population 14 million
Capital Baghdad
Currency 1000 Fils = 1 Iraqi dinar

Team
Manager Jorge Vieira   *Player to watch* Ammattion

Team colours All green

Congratulations to Iraq for their first appearance in a World Cup final competition.

Korea Rep.

Country
Population 42 million
Capital Seoul
Currency 100 Jeon = 1 Won

Team
Manager Kim Jung-Nam   *Player to watch* Choi Soon-Ho

Team colours All red

Previous appearances in finals One previous appearance as Korea.

Algeria

Country
Population 20 million
Capital Algiers
Currency 100 centimes = 1 Algerian dinar

Team
Manager Rabah Saadane   *Player to watch* Harkouk

Team colours Green and white

Previous appearances in finals
Algeria qualified in 1982 for the first time.

Morocco

Country
Population 20 million
Capital Rabat
Currency 100 centimes = 1 Dirham

Team
Manager Jose Faria   *Players to watch* Haddaoui, Timoumi

Team colours All red

Previous appearances in finals
This is Morocco's second appearance in the World Cup finals.

The Finals

Draw for the 1986 World Cup finals

There will be fifty-two matches in the final tournament and these will be played between 31st May and 29th June. The teams were put into the draw on 15th December 1985 and arranged in six groups of four. In each group the teams play each other once and a league table is drawn up from the results. The champions and runners-up from each group together with the four best third place teams make the sixteen teams for a knock-out competition. This will cover the second round, the quarter and semi-finals. The four semi-finalists will contest a place in the World Cup final or the third and fourth place play-off.

The winner of the final will become World Champions and qualify automatically for the 1990 competition in Italy.

How they line up

Seeded teams in *italic* type

GROUP A
Played in Puebla and Mexico City
1 *Italy*
2 Bulgaria
3 Argentina
4 Korea Rep.

GROUP B
Played in Mexico City and Toluca
5 *Mexico*
6 Belgium
7 Paraguay
8 Iraq

GROUP C
Played in Leon and Irapuato
9 *France*
10 Canada
11 USSR
12 Hungary

GROUP D
Played in Guadalajara and Monterrey
13 *Brazil*
14 Spain
15 Algeria
16 N. Ireland

GROUP E
Played in Queretaro and Nezahualcoyotl
17 *W. Germany*
18 Uruguay
19 Scotland
20 Denmark

GROUP F
Played in Monterrey and Guadalajara
21 *Poland*
22 Morocco
23 Portugal
24 England

1986 WORLD CUP FINALS IN MEXICO

Who will win this magnificent trophy? Place *your* prediction in the space below.

© FIFA 1974

Now follow the 24 teams through the final stages of the competition.
By filling in all the results in the spaces provided, you will not only see whether your prediction was correct, you will also have created a lasting souvenir of the World Cup finals 1986.

Competition chart

*Start to fill in **after** first round*

First Round

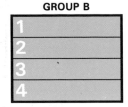

GROUP A

1
2
3
4

GROUP B

1
2
3
4

GROUP C

1
2
3
4

Second

Match 1 — 1 v 3

Match 2 — 1 v 3

Match 3 — 1 v 3

Match 4 — 1 v 3

Four best 3rd place teams

Quarter

Match *a*

Match 4 winner — v — Match 5 winner

Match *b*

Match 6 winner — v — Match 1 winner

Semi

Match *a* winner — v — Match *b* winner

The results of the draw
The colour coding shows how the winners, runners-up and four 3rd place teams with the best record, in each first round group, will progress through each round. For easy reference these colours are followed throughout this section of the book.
Complete this table as the tournament progresses.

League Tables

GROUP D	GROUP E	GROUP F
1	1	1
2	2	2
3	3	3
4	4	4

Round

Match 5

2
2

v

Match 6

1
2

v

Match 7

2
2

v

Match 8

1
2

v

Final

Match *c*

Match 8 winner	
Match 2 winner	

v

Match *d*

Match 3 winner	
Match 7 winner	

v

Final

Match *c* winner	
Match *d* winner	

v

3rd & 4th

v

Final

v

World Cup diary

FIRST ROUND

31st MAY
Bulgaria v Italy *(A)*

1st JUNE
Canada v France *(C)*
Spain v Brazil *(D)*

2nd JUNE
Argentina v Korea Rep. *(A)*
USSR v Hungary *(C)*
Morocco v Poland *(F)*

3rd JUNE
Belgium v Mexico *(B)*
Algeria v Northern Ireland *(D)*
Portugal v England *(F)*

4th JUNE
Paraguay v Iraq *(B)*
Uruguay v West Germany *(E)*
Scotland v Denmark *(E)*

5th JUNE
Italy v Argentina *(A)*
Korea Rep. v Bulgaria *(A)*
France v USSR *(C)*

6th JUNE
Hungary v Canada *(C)*
Brazil v Algeria *(D)*
England v Morocco *(F)*

7th JUNE
Mexico v Paraguay *(B)*
Northern Ireland v Spain *(D)*
Poland v Portugal *(F)*

8th JUNE
Iraq v Belgium *(B)*
West Germany v Scotland *(E)*
Denmark v Uruguay *(E)*

9th JUNE
Hungary v France *(C)*
USSR v Canada *(C)*

10th JUNE
Korea Rep. v Italy *(A)*
Argentina v Bulgaria *(A)*

11th JUNE
Iraq v Mexico *(B)*
Paraguay v Belgium *(B)*
Portugal v Morocco *(F)*
England v Poland *(F)*

12th JUNE
Northern Ireland v Brazil *(D)*
Algeria v Spain *(D)*

13th JUNE
Denmark v West Germany *(E)*
Scotland v Uruguay *(E)*

Letters in italic denote groups.
The map shows where the
different groups will play.

SECOND ROUND

15th JUNE
Match 1 – B winner v A or C or D third
Match 2 – C winner v A or B or F third

16th JUNE
Match 3 – A winner v C or D or E third
Match 4 – D winner v B or E or F third

17th JUNE
Match 5 – A second v C second
Match 6 – F winner v E second

18th JUNE
Match 7 – F second v B second
Match 8 – E winner v D second

QUARTER FINALS

21st JUNE
Match *a* –
Match 4 winners v Match 5 winners
Match *b* –
Match 6 winners v Match 1 winners

22nd JUNE
Match *c* –
Match 8 winners v Match 2 winners
Match *d* –
Match 3 winners v Match 7 winners

SEMI-FINALS

25th JUNE
Match *a* winners v Match *b* winners
Match *c* winners v Match *d* winners

THIRD/FOURTH PLACE
PLAY-OFF – 28th JUNE

WORLD CUP FINAL – 29th JUNE

FIRST ROUND
GROUP A

Italy

Bulgaria

Argentina

Korea Rep.

Mural at the stadium in Puebla

Opening Match 31st May *at Azteca Stadium, Mexico City*	**Bulgaria** Score ☐	**Italy**	Score ☐
2nd June *at Olimpico '68 Stadium, Mexico City*	**Argentina** ☐	**Korea Rep.**	☐
5th June *at Cuahtémoc Stadium, Puebla*	**Italy** ☐	**Argentina**	☐
5th June *at Olimpico '68 Stadium, Mexico City*	**Korea Rep.** ☐	**Bulgaria**	☐
10th June *at Cuahtémoc Stadium, Puebla*	**Korea Rep.** ☐	**Italy**	☐
10th June *at Olimpico '68 Stadium, Mexico City*	**Argentina** ☐	**Bulgaria**	☐

Now fill in the results table: 2 points for a win; 1 point for a draw

	Won	Drawn	Lost	Goals for	Goals against	Points	
							A1
							A2
							A3

*Enter **A1** on page 47 and **A2** on page 48 in the second round.*
*If **A3** qualifies for the second round enter on page 47.*

41

FIRST ROUND
GROUP B

Mexico
Belgium
Paraguay
Iraq

Bomberona Stadium in Toluca

	Score		Score
3rd June **Belgium** *at Azteca Stadium, Mexico City*	☐	Mexico	☐
4th June **Paraguay** *at Bomberona Stadium, Toluca*	☐	Iraq	☐
7th June **Mexico** *at Azteca Stadium, Mexico City*	☐	Paraguay	☐
8th June **Iraq** *at Bomberona Stadium, Toluca*	☐	Belgium	☐
11th June **Iraq** *at Azteca Stadium, Mexico City*	☐	Mexico	☐
11th June **Paraguay** *at Bomberona Stadium, Toluca*	☐	Belgium	☐

Now fill in the results table: 2 points for a win; 1 point for a draw

	Won	Drawn	Lost	Goals for	Goals against	Points	
							B1
							B2
							B3

*Enter **B1** on page 47 and **B2** on page 48 in the second round.*
*If **B3** qualifies for the second round enter on page 47.*

FIRST ROUND
GROUP C
France
Canada
USSR
Hungary

City of León

	Score		Score
1st June Canada *at Nuevocampo Stadium, León*	☐	France	☐
2nd June USSR *at Revolucion Stadium, Irapuato*	☐	Hungary	☐
5th June France *at Nuevocampo Stadium, León*	☐	USSR	☐
6th June Hungary *at Revolucion Stadium, Irapuato*	☐	Canada	☐
9th June Hungary *at Nuevocampo Stadium, León*	☐	France	☐
9th June USSR *at Revolucion Stadium, Irapuato*	☐	Canada	☐

Now fill in the results table: 2 points for a win; 1 point for a draw

	Won	Drawn	Lost	Goals for	Goals against	Points	

Enter **C1** *on page 47 and* **C2** *on page 48 in the second round.*
If **C3** *qualifies for the second round enter on page 47.*

FIRST ROUND
GROUP D

Brazil

Spain

Algeria

N. Ireland

Guadalajara

	Score		Score

1st June **Spain** ☐ Brazil ☐
at Jalisco Stadium, Guadalajara

3rd June **Algeria** ☐ N. Ireland ☐
at 3 de Marzo Stadium, Guadalajara

6th June **Brazil** ☐ Algeria ☐
at Jalisco Stadium, Guadalajara

7th June **N. Ireland** ☐ Spain ☐
at 3 de Marzo Stadium, Guadalajara

12th June **N. Ireland** ☐ Brazil ☐
at Jalisco Stadium, Guadalajara

12th June **Algeria** ☐ Spain ☐
at Tecnológico Stadium, Monterrey

Now fill in the results table: 2 points for a win; 1 point for a draw

	Won	Drawn	Lost	Goals for	Goals against	Points	

*Enter **D1** on page 47 and **D2** on page 48 in the second round.*
*If **D3** qualifies for the second round enter on page 47.*

W. Germany
Uruguay
Scotland
Denmark

Corregidora Stadium, Querétaro

	Score		Score

4th June **Uruguay** ☐ W. Germany ☐
at Corregidora Stadium, Querétaro

4th June **Scotland** ☐ Denmark ☐
at Neza '86 Stadium, Nezahualcoyotl

8th June **W. Germany** ☐ Scotland ☐
at Corregidora Stadium, Querétaro

8th June **Denmark** ☐ Uruguay ☐
at Neza '86 Stadium, Nezahualcoyotl

13th June **Denmark** ☐ W. Germany ☐
at Corregidora Stadium, Querétaro

13th June **Scotland** ☐ Uruguay ☐
at Neza '86 Stadium, Nezahualcoyotl

Now fill in the results table: 2 points for a win; 1 point for a draw

	Won	Drawn	Lost	Goals for	Goals against	Points	
							E1
							E2
							E3

*Enter **E1** and **E2** on page 48 in the second round.*
*If **E3** qualifies for the second round enter on page 47.*

FIRST ROUND
GROUP F

Poland

Morocco

Portugal

England

Tecnológico Stadium, Monterrey

	Score		Score
2nd June Morocco *at Universitario Stadium, Monterrey*	☐	Poland	☐
3rd June Portugal *at Tecnológico Stadium, Monterrey*	☐	England	☐
6th June England *at Tecnológico Stadium, Monterrey*	☐	Morocco	☐
7th June Poland *at Universitario Stadium, Monterrey*	☐	Portugal	☐
11th June Portugal *at 3 de Marzo Stadium, Guadalajara*	☐	Morocco	☐
11th June England *at Universitario Stadium, Monterrey*	☐	Poland	☐

Now fill in the results table: 2 points for a win; 1 point for a draw

	Won	Drawn	Lost	Goals for	Goals against	Points	
							F1
							F2
							F3

*Enter **F1** and **F2** on page 48 in the second round.*
*If **F3** qualifies for the second round enter on page 47.*

SECOND ROUND

DO NOT FILL IN THIS PAGE UNTIL ALL FIRST ROUND MATCHES HAVE BEEN PLAYED.
FIXTURES FOR THIRD PLACE TEAMS WILL BE ANNOUNCED.

Match 1

at Azteca Stadium, Mexico City Sunday 15th June

Score

(B1).................... ☐

A3
C3 .... ☐
D3

Score

*Enter winners on line **1** in the quarter finals on page 49.*

Match 2

at Nuevocampo Stadium, León Sunday 15th June

Score

(C1).................... ☐

A3
B3 .... ☐
F3

Score

*Enter winners on line **2** in the quarter finals on page 50.*

Match 3

at Cuahtémoc Stadium, Puebla Monday 16th June

Score

(A1).................... ☐

C3
D3 .... ☐
E3

Score

*Enter winners on line **3** in the quarter finals on page 50.*

Match 4

at Jalisco Stadium, Guadalajara Monday 16th June

Score

(D1).................... ☐

B3
E3 .... ☐
F3

Score

*Enter winners on line **4** in the quarter finals on page 49.*

SECOND ROUND

Match 5

at Olimpico '68 Stadium, Mexico City Tuesday 17th June

Score

(A2).....................

Score

(C2).....................

Enter winners on line 5 in the quarter finals on page 49.

Match 6

at Universitario Stadium, Monterrey Tuesday 17th June

Score

(F1).....................

Score

(E2).....................

Enter winners on line 6 in the quarter finals on page 49.

Match 7

at Azteca Stadium, Mexico City Wednesday 18th June

Score

(F2).....................

Score

(B2).....................

Enter winners on line 7 in the quarter finals on page 50.

Match 8

at Corregidora Stadium, Querétaro Wednesday 18th June

Score

(E1).....................

Score

(D2).....................

Enter winners on line 8 in the quarter finals on page 50.

QUARTER FINALS

Match *a*

at Jalisco Stadium, Guadalajara   Saturday 21st June

Score

Score

4 .... ☐   5 .... ☐

*Enter winners on line **a** in the semi-finals on page 51.*

Match *b*

at Universitario Stadium, Monterrey   Saturday 21st June

Score

Score

6 .... ☐   1 .... ☐

*Enter winners on line **b** in the semi-finals on page 51.*   49

QUARTER FINALS

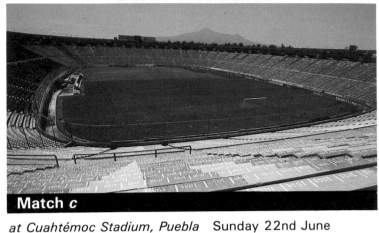

Match c

at Cuahtémoc Stadium, Puebla   Sunday 22nd June

Score

8 .... ☐   2 .... ☐

*Enter winners on line **c** in the semi-finals on page 51.*

Match d

at Azteca Stadium, Mexico City   Sunday 22nd June

Score

3 .... ☐   7 .... ☐

*Enter winners on line **d** in the semi-finals on page 51.*

SEMI-FINALS

at Azteca Stadium, Mexico City Wednesday 25th June

Score

a. . . . . ☐

Score

b. . . . . ☐

Goal Scorers:

Goal Scorers:

Enter winners in the final overleaf.
Enter losers in the 3rd place play-off overleaf.

Rossi (20) of Italy, scoring in the 1982 semi-final against Poland

at Jalisco Stadium, Guadalajara Wednesday 25th June

Score

c. . . . . ☐

Score

d. . . . . ☐

Goal Scorers:

Goal Scorers:

Enter winners in the final overleaf.
Enter losers in the 3rd place play-off overleaf.

THIRD AND FOURTH PLACE PLAY-OFF

Saturday 28th June
at Cuahtémoc Stadium, Puebla

Score

.... ☐

Players:

Score

.... ☐

Players:

Substitutes:

Substitutes:

Goal Scorers:

Goal Scorers:

Winners........................... take 3rd place

Losers........................... take 4th place